ULTIMATE SLIME GUIDE

SARAH McCLELLAND

LITTLE BINS FOR LITTLE HANDS

SLIME OF A DEDICATION

This crazy book of slime is dedicated to my awesome son, who sparked all the creativity (and then some) that you will find within these pages.

~Mom

Copyright © 2018 Sarah McClelland, Little Bins of Little Hands.
https://www.littlebinsforlittlehands.com

All rights reserved. No portion of this book may be reproduced in any form without permission from the author.

Book jacket and interior design created by Marie C Tucker Graphic Design. Printed by CreateSpace, an Amazon.com Company.

DISCLAIMER
The activities in this book are intended to be done under adult supervision. Appropriate and reasonable caution should be taken at all times. Please read our slime safety notes very carefully. The author of this book disclaims all liability for any damage, mishap, or injury that may occur from engaging in any of the activities in this book.

TABLE OF SLIME-TENTS

A SLIMY DEDICATION 2
TABLE OF SLIME-TENTS 3-5
A SLIMY INTRODUCTION 7
SLIME MAKING SAFETY TIPS 8
SLIME TROUBLESHOOTING 9

SLIMIEST SUPPLIES

BASIC SLIME MAKING SUPPLIES 10
SLIME STORAGE 11
THE FUN PART, SLIME MIX-INS 12-13

BASIC SLIME MAKING RECIPES

BASIC SLIME RECIPES INTRO 14
LIQUID STARCH SLIME 16-19
SALINE SOLUTION SLIME 20-23
FLUFFY SALINE SLIME 24-27
CLASSIC BORAX SLIME 28-31

UNIQUE SLIME RECIPES

UNIQUE SLIME RECIPES INTRO 32
BUBBLEGUM SLIME 34
BUTTER SLIME 35
CALMING LAVENDER SLIME 36
CLAY SLIME 37
CRUNCHY SLIMES 38-39
EXTREME GLITTER SLIME 40
FIDGET SLIME 41
FOAM BEAD SLIMES 42-43
GALAXY SLIME 44
GLOW IN THE DARK SLIME 45
GOLD & SILVER SLIME 46
LIQUID GLASS SLIME 47

TABLE OF SLIME-TENTS

UNIQUE SLIME RECIPES (continued)
- MAGNETIC SLIME 48
- MERMAID SLIME 49
- RAINBOW SLIME 50
- SAND & FLUFF SLIME 51
- SANDY BEACH SLIME 52
- SCENTED SLIME 53
- SNOW SLIMES 54-55
- UNICORN SLIME 56
- WATER BEADS SLIME 57

SEASONAL SLIME RECIPES
- SEASONAL SLIMES INTRODUCTION 58
- NEW YEAR'S SLIMES 60
- CELEBRATION SLIMES 61
- WINTER SLIMES 62-63
- VALENTINE'S DAY SLIMES 64-65
- ST. PATRICK'S DAY SLIMES 66-67
- EASTER SLIMES 68-69
- EARTH DAY SLIMES 70-71
- SPRING SLIMES 72-73
- FOURTH OF JULY SLIMES 74
- SUMMER SLIMES 75-76
- BACK TO SCHOOL SLIMES 77
- AUTUMN SLIMES 78-79
- HALLOWEEN SLIMES 80-81
- THANKSGIVING SLIMES 82
- HANUKKAH SLIMES 83
- CHRISTMAS SLIMES 84-85

IMAGINATION STATION
- KITCHEN SINK SLIME! 86
- WE AREN'T JUST SLIME! 87

You can find even more slime, plus handy printables and videos *online!*

WWW.LITTLEBINSFORLITTLEHANDS.COM

SEE THIS ICON?

▶

THERE'S A VIDEO!

Slimes on front cover from left to right: Fall Leaves Slime pg 79, Fluffy Saline Slime pgs 26-27, Planet Earth Slime pg 71.
Slimes on back cover from left to right: New Year's Eve Party Slime pg 60, Glow Slime pg 45, Crunchy Slime pgs 38-39.

A SLIMY INTRODUCTION

Slime is a rich, textural experience for the senses.

▶ Fluffy Saline Slime, page 26-27

A SLIMY INTRODUCTION

Our homemade slime making journey began several years ago around Halloween time. Who doesn't love anything that oozes and is creepy and gooey at Halloween? We do! We do! What we love the most about slime is all the fun themes you can add for holidays, seasons, special occasions, favorite characters, favorite movies, and any theme your imagination can dream up.

Over the course of the past four years, my son Liam and I have worked with our slime recipes to perfect them. And like any good cookie recipe, some things take a little practice to get right. Your slime may not be picture perfect the first time you make it, but our recipes will set you up for awesome slime, so try again!

Slime is an awesome science activity with a fun chemical reaction which makes slime a cool hands-on learning experience! Slime adds so much value to play. Whether you are making a moldable slime, an extra-squishy slime, or a fluffy slime, kids have the opportunity to immerse themselves in highly engaging, tactile, sensory play. If you love to play with different textures, and know kids who do too, this is the book for you.

I hope the recipes from this *Ultimate Slime Guide* spark your creativity and inspire your own slime recipes!

Happy slime making to all!

~Sarah and Liam

SLIME MAKING SAFETY TIPS

Slime is super fun to make, but it's still important to keep basic safety tips and practices in mind!

Adult supervision is always recommended. Children should always have adult supervision when making slime. I also recommend adults measure the slime activators (borax, liquid starch, saline solution), especially for younger kids.

Making slime is a science experiment, and a very cool one too! You might think that slime is just something really neat to play with, and you're totally right! BUT, slime is also chemistry! Like any cool chemistry experiment, you are working with different ingredients and mixtures that create reactions. All slime activities should be **properly cleaned up afterwards**. Disinfect surfaces, mixing tools, bowls, and any containers.

Wash hands thoroughly after playing with slime and remind kids to not touch their face while playing with their slime. It's also best to keep slime out of hair, off clothes, and away from furniture and rugs! We play with our slime at the kitchen counter, table, or on a cookie sheet to contain the mess and stay safe.

Do not switch out ingredients if it is not suggested or listed. This can result in an unwanted chemical reaction. It's never a good idea to substitute the correct ingredients with incorrect ones just to see what happens. Be safe!

Most slimes contain some form of borax or ingredients from the boron family (such as boric acid or sodium borate) which is commonly found in liquid starch, saline solution, contact solution, and eye drops. While we have never experienced skin sensitivities using our Basic Slime Recipes, every person's skin is different. Please use your best judgement as to whether or not slime making is safe for you and your family. You can use disposable gloves if you are concerned with skin sensitivity.

SLIME TROUBLESHOOTING

What happens when my slime fails?

So you have a slime fail on your hands, a big gloppy mess, and you are wondering what to do about it. For the most part, these slime fails can not be fixed. The best thing to do is start over with your slime. Here's why:

REASONS FOR A SLIME FAILURE

1. You didn't use the right type of glue.
Make sure you are using a PVA (polyvinyl acetate) glue.

2. You did not use the right slime activator or the correct amounts. Your saline solution should contain both the ingredients sodium borate and boric acid. Liquid starch comes in a bottle. You can not substitute homemade recipes for either of these.

3. You didn't read the directions thoroughly, and the steps weren't followed correctly and/or the ingredients weren't measured correctly.

4. You added way too much large size confetti. This will disrupt the oozing of the slime and cause your slime to break more easily.

5. Kneading is really important to improving the texture of your slime. It also helps to reduce the stickiness particularly in the Fluffy and Saline Solution Slime Recipes.

6. If your slime is still incredibly sticky and you have kneaded it thoroughly, add more slime activator a drop at a time. But add too much and your slime will become stiff quickly!

7. You gave up! Don't be afraid to try again. You can learn by watching videos on how to make slime at www.LittleBinsForLittleHands.com! If you see a "play" icon in the bottom right corner of slime photo, there's a video of that slime recipe online. Link to all our videos here.

Go forth and make awesome slime!

BASIC SLIME MAKING SUPPLIES

To make our four Basic Slime Recipes, you need to stock up on the best slime making supplies and tools! You can generally pick up these ingredients at your local grocery store or big box store. Because we love slime so much, we buy both our clear glue and white glue by the gallon.

Visit www.LittleBinsforLittleHands.com Our "Recommended Slime Supplies Resource Page" has a more specific list of supplies, as well as a printable "Slime Supplies Checklist." Print it out and take it with you to the store. Or keep it handy when you need to stock up.
Link: Recommended Slime Supplies & Slime Supplies Checklist

MIXING TOOLS
Medium or large size mixing bowls · Measuring cups · Measuring spoons · Spoons

BASIC INGREDIENTS
White & clear washable PVA school glue · Water · Food Coloring · Shaving Cream

SLIME ACTIVATORS
Baking Soda · Saline Solution* · Borax Powder · Liquid Starch
   *Sodium borate & boric acid MUST be ingredients!

SLIME STORAGE

You can keep your homemade slime for quite awhile, if you store it properly. Slime needs to stay covered or else it will dry out. If slime is stored correctly it can last for weeks, but you will probably want to make a new one before that!

When it comes to storing our slime recipes you have several options.

SUPPLY LIST
For short and long term storage try one of these options:

- Plastic Craft Jars
- Novelty Jars
- Mason Jars
- Baby Food Jars
- Reusable Plastic or Glass Containers
- Recycled Deli Containers
- Condiment Cups
- Clear Plastic Ornaments

Slime is an awesome party activity. Let your guests make their own slime! Set up a slime mix-ins buffet of glitter, confetti, and more.

Slime is great for party favors too! You can add fun labels to your slime containers. We offer several sizes of printable slime labels. Find our printable slime labels here.

THE SLIMIEST SUPPLIES

THE FUN PART, SLIME MIX-INS

Go beyond everyday slimes and create cool themed slime! Use food coloring, different types of glitter, themed confetti, table scatter, or even small plastic accessories.

There are glitters for every occasion! We have used regular glitter, tinsel glitter, neon glitter, holographic glitter, and gold and silver glitter to make cool slime themes come to life and really sparkle.

Confetti is available for every celebration! Keep an eye out for seasonal and holiday confetti such as leaves, turkeys, feathers, bats, pumpkins, snowflakes, dreidels, hearts, shamrocks, leprechauns, Easter eggs, bunnies, smiley faces, butterflies, stars, or balloons.

It doesn't stop at glitter and confetti! We use polystyrene foam beads, plastic fishbowl beads, pony beads, and water beads! Try adding colored sand for texture or beach sand from a favorite beach along with a few seashells. Plastic spiders, animals, plastic building bricks, or gems are also great to add to a slime to create a fun theme. Just make sure what you add is/are perfectly washable or easily replaceable. I am always keeping an eye out for themed accessories to add to our slime recipes. Craft stores and dollar stores are perfect places to find these fun additions.

MIX-INS SUPPLY LIST

Confetti	Fishbowl Beads	Colored Craft Sand
Sequins	Slushy Beads	Iron Oxide Powder
Glitter	Water Beads	Glow Powder
Gems	Mini Plastic Items	Gelatin Powder
Pony Beads	Mini Erasers	Instant or Fake Snow
Alphabet Beads	Pebbles	Soft Clay
Foam Beads	Seashells	Acrylic Paints
Sugar Beads	Beach Sand	Liquid Fragrance

THE SLIMIEST SUPPLIES

AN INTRODUCTION TO BASIC SLIME RECIPES

Our four foundational Basic Slime Recipes in this section are the foundations for all of our Unique and Seasonal Slime Recipes! I will refer back to these pages in those sections. Because these Basic Slime Recipes are so important to making awesome slime, I have laid them out for you with step by step instructions and photographs. You will also find some helpful tips along the way. Remember, you may have to give these slime recipes a few tries to get them just right.

We have used these Basic Slime Recipes for well over 500 batches of super cool slime. In the following sections you will have the chance to "dress up" your slimes using food coloring, glitter, confetti, and fun mix-ins to create awesome themes or just amazing swirls of color.* Use these Basic Slime Recipes to create wild slimes you and your kids will love to play with over and over again!

The BEST slimes start with these Basic Slime Recipes!

*One note about swirling colors: Eventually the colors will blend together. Rainbow Slime (found in pg 50) looks super cool, but as you squish it and play with it, the slime will become a brownish color. However, if you use shades of a similar color, such as the colors in our Under the Sea Slime (found on pg 76), the colors will work more harmoniously with each other as they mix together.

Rainbow Slime, page 50

BASIC SLIME MAKING RECIPES

LIQUID STARCH SLIME RECIPE

Our Liquid Starch Slime Recipe is truly the quickest slime to whip up, and so easy to customize.

BASIC SLIME MAKING RECIPES

LIQUID STARCH SLIME RECIPE

Initially your slime might appear stringy and very unlike the photos, but it will come together as you knead it.

TIP: After mixing your slime, transfer it to a clean and dry container. Let it sit for 5 minutes before kneading. For thicker slime try adding a ½ cup of liquid starch.

STEP 1
Measure ½ cup of white or clear PVA glue into bowl.

STEP 2
Add ½ cup of water and stir.

BASIC SLIME MAKING RECIPES

STEP 3

Add food coloring (mix-ins too if you wish) and stir.

STEP 4

Add ¼ cup of liquid starch.

STEP 5

Stir until it becomes too difficult with a spoon or craft stick. This slime will start to form instantly.

STEP 6

Pick up the slime with your hands and knead until smooth.

SALINE SOLUTION SLIME RECIPE

We have really been enjoying the awesome stretchiness of our Saline Solution Slime Recipe.

BASIC SLIME MAKING RECIPES

SALINE SOLUTION SLIME RECIPE

Give this slime a good quick stir to get it to come together. If your slime is still too sticky after kneading it for a few minutes, add a few drops of the saline solution and knead some more.

TIP: For a stretchier slime reduce saline solution to ½ tbsp. Alternatively, you can add more baking soda for a thicker putty-like slime.

STEP 1

Measure ½ cup of white or clear PVA glue into bowl.

STEP 2

Add ½ cup of water and stir.

STEP 3

Add food coloring and stir. Sprinkle ¼ teaspoon of baking soda on the surface and gently stir into glue mixture.

STEP 4

Add your mix-ins now so that the baking soda doesn't stick to them. Add 1 tablespoon of saline solution.

STEP 5

Stir the mixture until it begins to pull away from the sides and bottom of the bowl.

STEP 6

Squirt a few drops of saline solution onto your hands. Pick up the slime and knead until smooth.

BASIC SLIME MAKING RECIPES

FLUFFY SALINE SLIME RECIPE

Fluffy Saline Solution Slime is like playing with a cloud. It has an amazing texture!

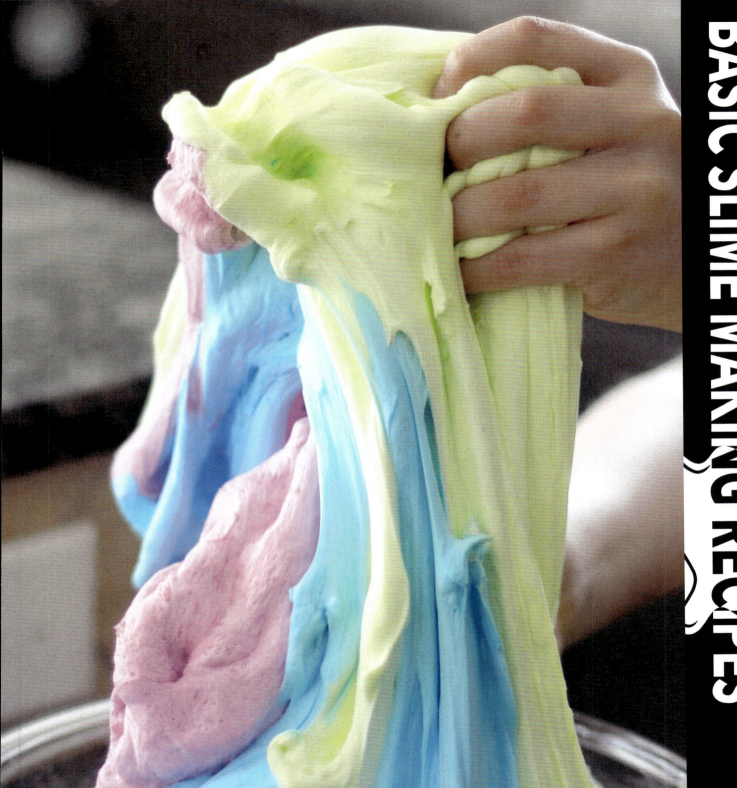

FLUFFY SALINE SLIME RECIPE

Make sure to choose a bowl big enough for all the ingredients. Give it a good quick stir to get it to come together. Make sure to knead your slime well before adding more solution if it seems too sticky.

TIP: You can experiment with using less foam shaving cream for a stretchier, fluffy slime.

STEP 1
In a bowl, put 3-4 cups of foam shaving cream and some food coloring. Gently stir to incorporate.

STEP 2
Measure ½ cup of white or clear PVA glue into the bowl and gently stir.

STEP 3

Sprinkle ¼-½ teaspoon of baking soda on the surface and gently stir into mixture.

STEP 4

Add 1 tablespoon of saline solution.

STEP 5

Stir the fluffy mass until it begins to pull away from the sides and bottom of the bowl.

STEP 6

Squirt a few drops of saline solution onto your hands. Pick up the slime and knead until smooth.

CLASSIC BORAX SLIME RECIPE

If you want crystal clear slime that looks like liquid glass, our Classic Borax Slime Recipe is the best!

BASIC SLIME MAKING RECIPES

CLASSIC BORAX SLIME RECIPE

This is the classic slime recipe used in science class demonstrations. It's also the best for crystal clear slime.

TIP: This recipe works wonderfully with white PVA glue, but if you love adding confetti, using clear PVA glue will really make it pop!

STEP 1
Measure ½ cup of white or clear PVA glue into bowl.

STEP 2
Add ½ cup of water and stir.

BASIC SLIME MAKING RECIPES

STEP 3

Add food coloring, glitter, or confetti, of your choice.

STEP 4

In a separate bowl, make a borax solution by stirring ½ cup of warm water with ¼ tsp of borax powder.

STEP 5

Add the borax solution to the glue mixture and stir until all the solution is mixed in thoroughly.

STEP 6

Remove the slime from the bowl and knead until smooth.

UNIQUE SLIME RECIPES INTRODUCTION

Exciting Fun Cool Awesome
Amazing Extreme Unique
Interesting

All excellent ways to describe this section of slime recipes!
You have just read through some great Basic Slime Recipes, tips, and hints. I hope you have gotten your feet wet by trying out a couple recipes to see which is your favorite. Get ready to turn up the fun factor and add some unique twists!

How do I use the Unique Slime Recipes Section?

Glad you asked! Each of the following Unique Slime Recipes will use one of the Four Basic Slime Recipes as a foundation. I will indicate which one we used and suggest other recipes that will work as well. The Basic Slime Recipes allow you to easily customize and get creative.

You will also find suggestions for color choices, glitter, confetti options, and mix-in ideas to create the slime. Copy our exact theme or use it as a springboard to create your own unique slimes.

A few of these Unique Slime Recipes alter a Basic Slime Recipe or simply showcase a popular theme. The rest of them require one or two special items that make the slime extra unique. Special ingredients can be found in craft stores or online. Before you go to the store, make sure to check out our recommended slime supplies to see what we like to use!

Our Slime Supplies & Checklist.

UNIQUE SLIME RECIPES

Galaxy Slime, page 44

UNIQUE SLIME RECIPES

BUBBLEGUM SLIME

This cool slime looks and feels like bubble gum! It even makes the popping sounds you would get from blowing small bubbles. You may even see tiny bubbles when squashing and squeezing the slime!

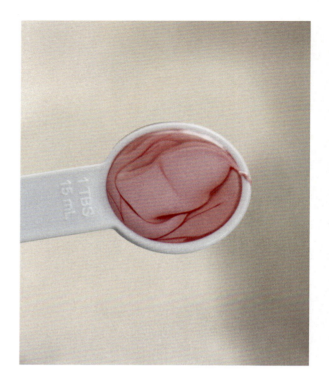

BASIC SLIME RECIPES:
Saline Solution Slime
Liquid Starch Slime
Classic Borax Slime
Clear or white PVA glue

MIX-INS:
Pink pearlized or metallic acrylic paint

SPECIAL STEP/TIP:
During the mix-ins step of the Basic Slime Recipe, mix in 1 tbsp of pink pearlized or metallic acrylic paint. Although the slime has a sheen to it, you can still add more glitter! There are lots of fun colors to try, so don't feel like you have to choose pink!

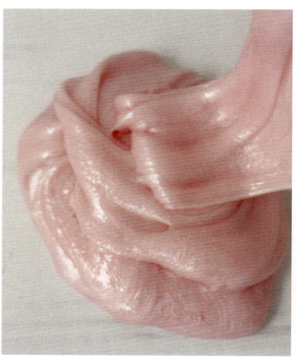

BUTTER SLIME

Here's a slime that's smooth, just like butter. It stretches like a dream, but it is still thick and soft with a nice texture. All you need to do is add one secret ingredient from the kitchen cabinet. Just remember, no tasting!

BASIC SLIME RECIPE:
Liquid Starch Slime
White PVA glue

MIX-INS:
Powdered cornstarch
Food coloring

SPECIAL STEP/TIP:
During the special mix-ins step, add a couple of tablespoons of powdered cornstarch and mix well! Give the kids a pretend or plastic butter knife to spread the slime or cut it into chunks for a dramatic experience.

UNIQUE SLIME RECIPES

CALMING LAVENDER SLIME

Slime is already an amazing and calming sensory play material for kids. Lavender is known for its relaxing and calming properties. Enjoy lavender slime in the evening, on sick days, or anytime for stress relief.

BASIC SLIME RECIPES:
Saline Solution Slime
Liquid Starch Slime
Classic Borax Slime
White PVA glue

MIX-INS:
Food coloring
Glitter
Lavender Fragrance Oil
Dried Lavender

SPECIAL STEP/TIP:
During the mix-ins step, add a drop or two of a lavender fragrance oil and continue with the basic slime recipe directions. You can even add dried lavender flowers to the slime once it is fully mixed!

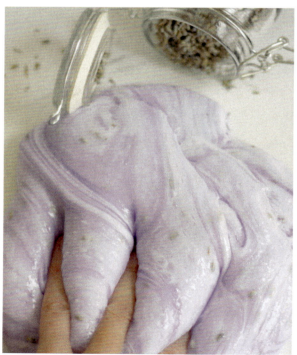

CLAY SLIME

Try this moldable slime that uses soft clay as an extra special ingredient!

BASIC SLIME RECIPES:
Saline Solution Slime
Liquid Starch Slime
Classic Borax Slime
White PVA glue

MIX-INS:
Food coloring
Soft modeling clay

SPECIAL STEP/TIP:
To make clay slime, start with a Basic Slime Recipe in a color that pairs well with color of your soft clay. Take 1 ounce of soft clay and flatten it out. Place it on your slime. Squish and knead the clay and slime together until they are fully incorporated.

There are several types of soft clay available. We use a denser clay which needs a smaller amount. You will need to use more if you purchased a less dense clay.

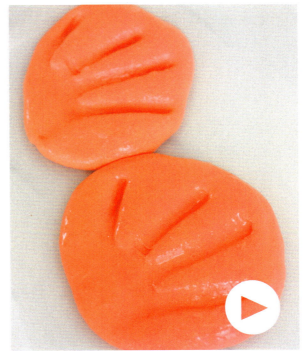

UNIQUE SLIME RECIPES

CRUNCHY SLIMES

Use a variety of acrylic beads to add texture to your homemade slime! We used three different shapes and sizes: fishbowl, sugar and slushy beads. These beads are commonly used as vase fillers.

BASIC SLIME RECIPES:
Liquid Starch Slime
Saline Solution Slime
Classic Borax Slime
Clear PVA glue

MIX-INS:
Food coloring if desired
Fishbowl beads
Slushy beads
Sugar beads

FISHBOWL BEAD RECIPE:
These are the largest of the three types of beads and create a bubbly texture in the slime. Fishbowl beads are generally clear but also come in a variety of translucent colors. Add a few plastic fish for an "under the sea" theme.

CRUNCHY SLIMES
(continued)

SLUSHY BEAD RECIPE:
Slushy beads are smaller than fishbowl beads and opaque in color. They add a fun slushy or smoothie appearance to your slime like finely chopped ice! Make your slime with bright or tropical colors for a summer slushy look.

SUGAR BEAD RECIPE:
Sugar beads are the smallest of the three types of acrylic beads and not quite as round. They add a fun granular texture to your slime.

SPECIAL STEP/TIP:
The more beads you add to your slime recipe, the denser the slime will become. I recommend adding a ½ cup of beads during the mix-ins step. Experiment with more or less beads to find your perfect amount.

EXTREME GLITTER SLIME

This is a super glittery and sparkly slime that makes any theme, holiday, or special occasion slime perfect. Make several batches of this slime in similar shades and swirl together for a cool effect.

BASIC SLIME RECIPES:
Saline Solution Slime
Liquid Starch Slime
Classic Borax Slime
Clear PVA glue

MIX-INS:
Food coloring
Glitter: fine, regular, tinsel, chunky

SPECIAL STEP/TIP:
To make Extreme Glitter Slime, use one of the three Basic Slime Recipes listed above.
Add desired food coloring, then add a VERY generous amount of regular or tinsel glitter where indicated in the recipe.

FIDGET SLIME

Fidget slime is tougher and thicker than our regular slime. It's a whole new way to play with slime! Use it as a fidget tool and take it with you! Pull it out when you need to take a brain break, relax, or de-stress.

BASIC SLIME RECIPE:
Classic Borax Slime
White PVA glue

MIX-INS:
Food coloring

SPECIAL STEP/TIP:
You will omit the water from step 2 of the Classic Borax Slime Recipe then continue with the slime making instructions. Additionally, you don't need to make as much of this slime for one person. Cut the recipe in ½ if desired. Or divide the full recipe and make several colors.

UNIQUE SLIME RECIPES

FOAM BEAD SLIMES

Fun, textured, moldable slime is loads of fun! Add tiny foam beads in all colors for an extra squishy slime recipe. Use either white or clear glue for different looks!

BASIC SLIME RECIPES:
Liquid Starch Slime
Classic Borax Slime
Saline Solution Slime
White PVA glue
Clear PVA glue

MIX-INS:
Food coloring
Foam beads

CLEAR GLUE RECIPE:
Rainbow foam beads in varying sizes work well with clear glue. Add 1 cup of rainbow foam beads during the mix-ins step. For a clear slime look use the Classic Borax Slime Recipe. If you're using larger foam beads, you may want to add fewer beads.

FOAM BEAD SLIMES
(continued)

WHITE GLUE RECIPE:
White foam beads work well with white glue and food coloring. Add 1 cup of foam beads during the mix-ins step for basic slime recipe.

SPECIAL STEP/TIP:
For a looser crunchy foam slime use less foam beads. Experiment to find your favorite amount of foam beads. Add just a handful or the whole cup!

Use you favorite color foam beads or mix a rainbow of colors for a birthday cake themed slime!

For a stiffer, moldable foam slime, use the Classic Borax Slime Recipe. Omit water from Step 2, add 1 cup of beads, and continue with the slime recipe. This will make for a much stiffer foam slime that holds its shape!

GALAXY SLIME

Beautiful colors twist together to create an amazing galaxy in your hands.

BASIC SLIME RECIPES:
Saline Solution Slime
Liquid Starch Slime
Classic Borax Slime
Clear PVA glue

MIX-INS:
Food coloring
Silver glitter

SPECIAL STEP/TIP:
Make 4-5 small batches of the slime in different galaxy colors like black, orange, pink, blue and purple.

You can make a ½ batch of each to save on ingredients. Lay out your strips of slime in a row next to one another then twist into your galaxy slime.

GLOW IN THE DARK SLIME

Turn off the lights for this Glow in the Dark Slime! One extra ingredient makes for an out of this world experience!

BASIC SLIME RECIPES:
Saline Solution Slime
Liquid Starch Slime
Classic Borax Slime
Clear PVA glue

MIX-INS:
Glow in the dark pigment powder

SPECIAL STEP/TIP:
During the mix-ins step of the Basic Slime Recipe, add ½ tbsp of glow in the dark pigment powder. There is no need to add additional food coloring. Use the sunlight to "charge" your slime during the day or a try a flashlight to "charge" your slime at night. Take your slime into a dark area to see it glow!

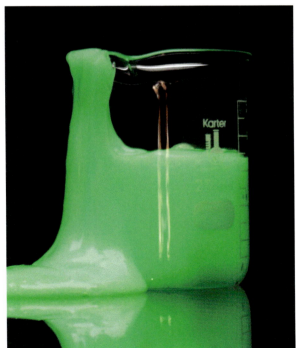

UNIQUE SLIME RECIPES

GOLD & SILVER SLIME

Whether you want a princess theme or you have a kid that loves to study precious metals, this glittering metallic Gold & Silver Slime twist together for sparkling awesomeness. Or you can make them individually and add fun items to fit your theme.

BASIC SLIME RECIPES:
Saline Solution Slime
Liquid Starch Slime
Classic Borax Slime
Clear PVA glue

MIX-INS:
Gold glitter glue
Gold glitter
Silver glitter glue
Silver glitter

SPECIAL STEP/TIP:
Add a 1oz bottle of glitter glue to the ½ cup measuring cup. You can easily find these at a dollar store! Fill remainder of ½ cup with clear glue for a total of ½ cup of glue. Continue with Basic Slime Recipe.

LIQUID GLASS SLIME

It is crystal clear like glass, so we call this Liquid Glass Slime.

BASIC SLIME RECIPES:
Classic Borax Slime
Alternative Slime*
Clear PVA glue

MIX-INS:
None, because it's clear as glass!

*ALTERNATIVE SLIME:
Use our Saline Solution Slime Recipe for reference here. The ingredients are the same, but mixed in a different order: Do STEP 1. Then, for STEP 2, in a separate bowl, mix the water (warm is best) & baking soda. Slowly poor that mixture into your clear glue and stir gently. Continue with STEPS 3-6.

SPECIAL STEP/TIP:
You will notice that your slime is initially filled with small air bubbles. Place your slime in a container and cover loosely. Set it aside for a few days. After that, the bubbles will have disappeared.

MAGNETIC SLIME

This slime acts like it's alive and is one of our most favorite slime recipes ever! You do need to have a special magnet called a neodymium magnet or rare earth magnet for the slime to work. Our favorite is the cube shaped one.

BASIC SLIME RECIPE:
Liquid Starch Slime
White PVA glue

MIX-INS:
Black iron oxide powder
Neodymium magnet

SPECIAL STEP/TIP:
After you have mixed the glue and water together, add ½ cup of black iron oxide powder and mix well. Continue with slime making directions. Your slime will deepen to a rich black color over time.

NOTE: Use a neodymium magnet to play with your slime, but DO NOT put magnets near electronics! Regular magnets are not powerful enough to move the slime.

MERMAID SLIME

A little like the magic mermaid bands, pillows, and blankets out there, our mermaid slime is a mix of shimmering colors and glitter.

BASIC SLIME RECIPES:
Saline Solution Slime
Liquid Starch Slime
Classic Borax Slime
Clear PVA glue

MIX-INS:
Food coloring
Regular glitter
Sequins

SPECIAL STEP/TIP:
We used teal, purple, and blue food coloring options to create a mermaid slime. Coordinate with glitter in a variety of sizes including fine, regular, or chunky! You can even add holographic sequins or confetti for an added shimmer. Add gems and seashells for play time.

UNIQUE SLIME RECIPES

RAINBOW SLIME

Kids will love making this enormous batch of Rainbow Slime. Go ahead and add glitter or sequins too! Note: The colors will eventually mix together leaving a muddy color, but you can think of a cool theme for that too!

BASIC SLIME RECIPES:
Saline Solution Slime
Liquid Starch Slime
Classic Borax Slime
Clear PVA glue

MIX-INS:
Food coloring
Glitter

SPECIAL STEP/TIP:
Because you will need to make 6 colored slimes, halve the recipes for each color. You can also add color coordinated glitter to each slime for even more sparkle! To make the rainbow, lay the colors out in a strip. Pick up the top of the strip and twist!

SAND & FLUFF SLIME

Fluffy slime combined with colored craft sand makes for an awesome new texture!

BASIC SLIME RECIPE:
Fluffy Saline Slime
White PVA glue

MIX-INS:
Food coloring
Colored craft sand

SPECIAL STEP/TIP:
First, mix shaving cream and food coloring in a bowl as directed. Next, add ½ cup of colored craft sand and stir to combine! Continue with fluffy slime directions. Make a few colors and swirl together for a fun effect!

You can also add colored craft sand to any of our Basic Slime Recipes for a fun alternative. Use white or clear PVA glue.

SANDY BEACH SLIME

Bring the beach home or take slime making outside. Grab a bucket of your favorite beach sand and turn it into slime! You can also use clean play sand.

BASIC SLIME RECIPE:
Liquid Starch Slime
Saline Solution Slime
Clear PVA glue

MIX-INS:
Beach sand or
Fine grain colored craft sand

SPECIAL STEP/TIP:
Add ¼ cup of beach or play sand during the mix in step of the Liquid Starch Slime Recipe. Add seashells, a small bucket, and even a small sand castle mold for play time. Try mixing your slime right in the sand bucket.

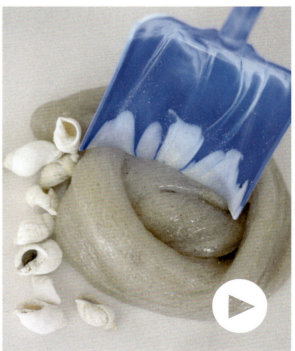

SCENTED SLIME

This is an easy way to make a fun, scented slime in your favorite flavor. We chose strawberry flavored gelatin for this scented slime. Just remember, no tasting!

BASIC SLIME RECIPE:
Saline Solution Slime
Clear PVA glue

MIX-INS:
Gelatin powder in any flavor
Food coloring if desired

SPECIAL STEP/TIP:
This Scented Slime Recipe is best if you use a ½ tsp of baking soda and 1 ½ tablespoons of saline solution. Sugar Free gelatin is not recommended.

Add 1 teaspoon of any flavored powdered gelatin after the glue and water have been mixed together. Food coloring can be added but is not necessary. Stir to combine and continue with the Saline Solution Slime Recipe instructions.

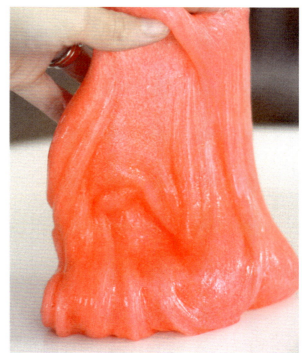

SNOW SLIMES

FAKE SNOW RECIPE:
A staple for winter decorating, fake snow is also perfect for creating an unusual slime texture even in the middle of summer.

BASIC SLIME RECIPES:
Liquid Starch Slime
Saline Solution Slime
Classic Borax Slime
White PVA glue

MIX-INS:
Food coloring
Fake plastic snow

SPECIAL STEP/TIP:
Look for a bag of finely shredded fake plastic snow for the best texture. Add a ½ cup of fake snow during the mix-ins step of the basic slime recipe.

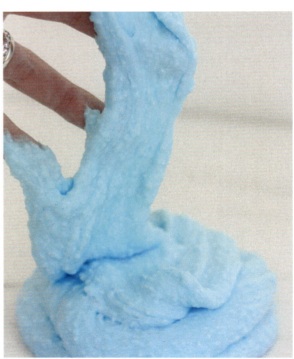

SNOW SLIMES
(continued)

INSTANT SNOW RECIPE:
Instant snow is fascinating to make on it's own (just add water), but it's even more fascinating when you add it to one of our Basic Slime Recipes! Perfect anytime of the year to add a cool texture to slime.

BASIC SLIME RECIPE:
Saline Solution Slime
Clear PVA glue

MIX-INS:
Food coloring
Instant snow

SPECIAL STEP/TIP:
Follow the directions on your instant snow package. Omit the ½ cup of water from Step 2 and replace with a ½ cup of instant snow. Continue with slime recipe. This slime can be stickier. Simply add a drop or two more of saline solution to lessen the stickiness.

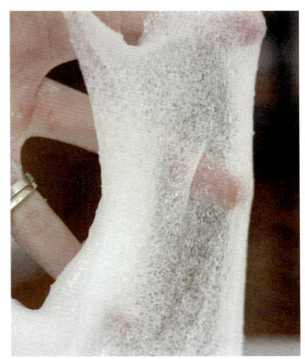

UNICORN SLIME

Unicorns are magical and so is this slime! Beautiful swirls of color with plenty of glitter let you make this slime as unique as an unicorn.

BASIC SLIME RECIPES:
Saline Solution Slime
Liquid Starch Slime
Classic Borax Slime
Clear or white PVA glue

MIX-INS:
Food coloring
Regular or tinsel glitter

SPECIAL STEP/TIP:
Unicorn Slime can be made with either clear or white glue for two gorgeous yet totally unique looks! White glue Unicorn Slime will be more pastel. Add glitter to the clear slime version for a real sparkle. We have printable unicorn slime labels and cards too! LINK

UNIQUE SLIME RECIPES

WATER BEAD SLIME

Water beads are so fun when added to your favorite Basic Slime Recipe! Make sure to allow time for them to plump up before making your slime.

BASIC SLIME RECIPES:
Saline Solution Slime
Liquid Starch Slime
Classic Borax Slime
Clear PVA glue

MIX-INS:
Fully plumped water beads
Food coloring if desired

SPECIAL STEP/TIP:
Water beads come in a small package and are very tiny to start. Follow the instructions on the package to get the beads nice and plump before adding them to the slime. During the mix-ins step of the Liquid Starch Slime Recipe, add ¼ cup of plump water beads.

Alternatively you can crush your water beads for a different texture!

SEASONAL SLIME RECIPE INTRODUCTION

Spooky Fun Winter Joyous Summer Festive Merry Autumn Holidays Creepy Seasons Spring

Seasonal themed slimes are perfect for celebrating and exploring the seasons and your favorite holidays. This section of Seasonal Slime Recipes lets you celebrate your favorite seasons and holidays in a new and creative way!

How do I use the Seasonal Slime Recipes Section?

Just like with the Unique Slime Recipes section (pgs 32-57), the following Seasonal Slime Recipes use one of the four foundational Basic Slime Recipes (pgs 14-31). These foundational recipes allow you to easily customize for each month of the year.

You will find our suggestions for color choices, glitter or confetti choices, and fun mix-in choices to create each slime. Copy our exact theme or use it as a springboard to create your own unique twist. I am always on the lookout for themed accessories to add to the play at dollar stores and craft stores.

Celebrations are often based on traditions, and traditions vary from home to home. You can create your own special slime using traditions from your favorite holiday memories or items that represent the season for you and your family.

SEASONAL SLIME RECIPES

Witch's Brew Fluffy Slime, page 80

NEW YEAR'S SLIME RECIPES

NEW YEAR'S EVE PARTY SLIME

Have a slime party with the colorful "POP!" of party crackers.

BASIC SLIME RECIPE:
Classic Borax Slime • Clear PVA glue

MIX-INS: Silver or gold glitter • Celebration confetti

SPECIAL STEP/TIP:
Add a burst of celebration confetti and a dash of glitter. Decorate the area with New Year's goodies like party beads, party poppers, and more!

CHINESE NEW YEAR SLIME

Red and gold are lucky colors because they convey happiness and prosperity in Chinese culture.

BASIC SLIME RECIPES:
Liquid Starch Slime • Saline Solution Slime • Classic Borax Slime • Clear PVA glue

MIX-INS: Red food coloring • Gold glitter • Gold sequins

SPECIAL STEP/TIP:
Add a few extra drops of red food coloring for a rich, red slime.

PARTY SLIME

Swirls of silver, gold, and rose gold make for an incredibly glittery party slime.

BASIC SLIME RECIPES: Liquid Starch Slime • Saline Solution Slime • Classic Borax Slime • Clear PVA glue

MIX-INS: Gold, silver & pink glitter • Gold party beads

SPECIAL STEP/TIP: Add your glitter combination during the mix-in step. No food coloring is required for this sparkling slime thanks to all that glitter!

MARDI GRAS SLIME

Celebrate Mardi Gras with homemade slime in the colorful hues of green, purple, and gold!

BASIC SLIME RECIPES: Liquid Starch Slime • Saline Solution Slime • Classic Borax Slime • Clear PVA glue

MIX-INS: Food coloring • Glitter • Sequins • Party beads

SPECIAL STEP/TIP: Make three batches of slime with purple, green, and gold glitter. Stretch the slime colors out and swirl together.

CELEBRATION SLIME RECIPES

WINTER SLIME RECIPES

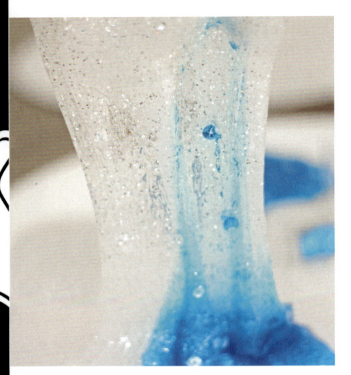

ICY SLIME

Jack Frost would be proud of this slime! Make glistening, icy slime perfect for snow day fun!

BASIC SLIME RECIPES:
Saline Solution Slime • Classic Borax Slime • Clear PVA glue

MIX-INS: Food coloring • Glitter • Sequins

SPECIAL STEP/TIP:
Make 2 batches of slime: one clear, one a bright icy blue! Add lots of glitter for sparkle. Swirl the two slimes together for an icy mix.

HOT CHOCOLATE SCENTED SLIME

Although this slime is NOT edible, it has the lovely smell of hot cocoa.

BASIC SLIME RECIPES:
Liquid Starch Slime • Saline Solution Slime • Classic Borax Slime • Clear or white PVA glue

MIX-INS: Hot cocoa mix packet

SPECIAL STEP/TIP:
Add the hot cocoa mix packet to your glue and water mixture. Stir thoroughly to combine and continue on with the Basic Slime Recipe.

WINTER SLIME RECIPES

MELTING SNOWMAN SLIME

Make a snowman out of slime instead of cold snow with this wintery slime.

BASIC SLIME RECIPES: Liquid Starch Slime • Saline Solution Slime • Classic Borax Slime • White PVA glue

MIX-INS: Silver glitter • Buttons

SPECIAL STEP/TIP: Make a batch of white slime and add silver glitter to make it sparkle. Add buttons and foam cut-outs to create a snowman. You can also add a snowman cookie cutter.

SNOWFLAKE SLIME

Glittering snowflake-filled slime is perfect for frozen, arctic, or wintery play.

BASIC SLIME RECIPE: Classic Borax Slime • Clear PVA glue

MIX-INS: Glitter • Snowflake confetti • Sequins

SPECIAL STEP/TIP: Use our Classic Borax Slime Recipe and add silver glitter along with white, silver, and translucent snowflake confetti or sequins for a winter storm in your slime!

VALENTINE'S DAY SLIME RECIPES

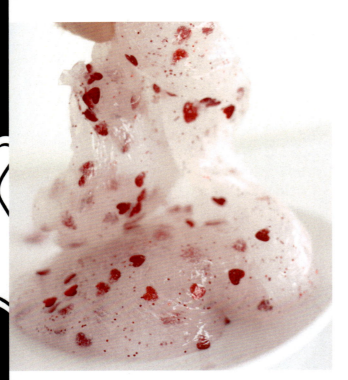

LOVE CONFETTI SLIME

Adding confetti hearts is a great way to make a Basic Slime Recipe into a slime filled with love!

BASIC SLIME RECIPES: Liquid Starch Slime • Saline Solution Slime • Classic Borax Slime • Clear PVA glue

MIX-INS: Red glitter • Heart confetti

SPECIAL STEP/TIP: To make your confetti really pop, use the Classic Borax Slime Recipe. Also try out the Liquid Glass Slime recipe (pg 47).

VALENTINE'S DAY FLUFFY SLIME

Fluffy swirls of red, pink, and purple are lovely for February slime!

BASIC SLIME RECIPE: Fluffy Saline Solution Slime • White PVA glue

MIX-INS: Red, pink & purple food coloring

SPECIAL STEP/TIP: Add heart shaped cookie cutters, plastic heart containers, or a plastic heart tray for fun Valentine's Day play! Once mixed, sprinkle glitter on top to make it sparkle!

VALENTINE'S DAY CRUNCHY SLIME

Use your favorite Valentine's Day colors and spread some love (and slime)!

BASIC SLIME RECIPE:
Crunchy Slime (pg 38-39)
• Clear or white PVA glue

MIX-INS: Purple & red food coloring • Foam beads (white or colored)

SPECIAL STEP/TIP:
Use equal parts foam beads to glue ratio. You can mix up your colored foam beads to get a confetti effect too!

VALENTINE'S DAY SWIRLED SLIME

Pick your favorite Valentine's Day colors to make your swirly slime.

BASIC SLIME RECIPES:
Liquid Starch Slime • Saline Solution Slime • Classic Borax Slime • Clear PVA glue

MIX-INS: Purple & red food coloring • Glitter • Heart confetti

SPECIAL STEP/TIP:
Make slimes in pink, purple, red, & clear with a Basic Slime Recipe. Set up a slime buffet of mix-ins to let the kids decorate their own slimes!

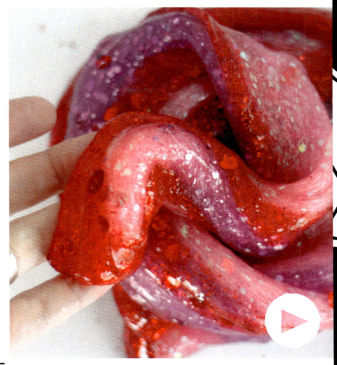

ST. PATRICK'S DAY SLIMES

LUCKY LEPRECHAUN SLIME

Leprechauns will love our shiny gold slime filled with gold coins!

BASIC SLIME RECIPES: Liquid Starch Slime • Saline Solution Slime • Classic Borax Slime • Clear PVA glue

MIX-INS: Yellow food coloring • Gold glitter • Plastic gold coins

SPECIAL STEP/TIP: Use lots of glitter for the most sparkle. Fill small black pots with this sparkly, coin filled slime for a lucky celebration!

SHAMROCK SLIME

Celebrate the luck of the Irish with shamrocks and clovers.

BASIC SLIME RECIPES: Liquid Starch Slime • Saline Solution Slime • Classic Borax Slime • Clear PVA glue

MIX-INS: Green glitter • Green & gold shamrock confetti

SPECIAL STEP/TIP: You can make batches of green slime and clear slime.
Add plenty of glitter and confetti. Then twist!

ST. PATRICK'S DAY SLIMES

FLUFFY FÁILTE SLIME

Whip up a batch of our Fluffy Saline Slime and fill it with glitter, gold, and sparkle.

BASIC SLIME RECIPE:
Fluffy Saline Solution Slime
• White PVA glue

MIX-INS: Food coloring
• Glitter • Confetti

SPECIAL STEP/TIP:
It's hard to achieve a bright green with fluffy slime, so you may need to add extra food coloring. Bury coins in your slime for a leprechaun treasure hunt!

IRISH EYES ARE SWIRLIN' SLIME

Go all out for St. Patrick's Day with a trio of bright and colorful slimes!

BASIC SLIME RECIPES:
Liquid Starch Slime • Saline Solution Slime • Classic Borax Slime • Clear PVA glue

MIX-INS: Glitter • Confetti • Coins • Plastic shamrocks

SPECIAL STEP/TIP:
Make 3 slimes with your favorite St. Patrick's Day colors: try Kelly green, glittering gold, or clear slime with green glitter. Make a swirl any leprechaun would love!

EASTER SLIME RECIPES

FLUFFY CHICK SLIME

Slime as fluffy as a baby chick's bottom.

BASIC SLIME RECIPES:
Fluffy Saline Solution Slime
• White PVA glue

MIX-INS: Yellow food coloring
• Glitter (optional)

SPECIAL STEP/TIP:
Baby chicks can be found at your local craft store. Some even have plastic feet you can stamp in your slime. Make fun chicky foot prints!

EGG-CELLENT SLIME

Fill your plastic Easter eggs with colorful slime for egg-citing play!

BASIC SLIME RECIPES:
Liquid Starch Slime • Saline Solution Slime • Classic Borax Slime • Clear or white PVA glue

MIX-INS: Food coloring
• Confetti • Glitter if desired

SPECIAL STEP/TIP:
Hide slime filled eggs for your Easter egg hunt! To make glitter show up best, use the clear glue slime.

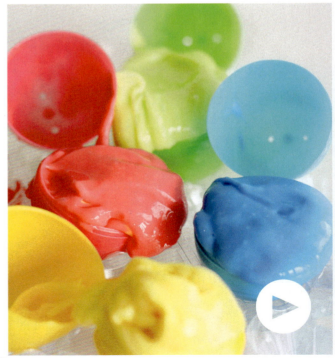

EGG ORNAMENT SLIME

Sparkly, glittery eggs make the perfect Easter decoration.

BASIC SLIME RECIPE:
Liquid Starch Slime • Saline Solution Slime • Classic Borax Slime • Clear or white PVA glue

MIX-INS: Food coloring • Glitter

SPECIAL STEP/TIP:
Look for refillable, clear plastic egg ornaments at your local craft store. For a tight seal, do not over fill egg ornaments.

BUNNIES, CHICKS & EGGS OH MY! SLIME

Your little chicks will burst with excitement over this slime! Fill clear slime with Easter themed confetti and glitter for sparkle.

BASIC SLIME RECIPE:
Classic Borax Slime • Clear PVA glue

MIX-INS: Easter confetti • Fine & chunky glitter • Easter sequins

SPECIAL STEP/TIP:
You can add food coloring to match or compliment your confetti.

EASTER SLIME RECIPES

EARTH DAY SLIME RECIPES

CRUNCHY EARTH SLIME

Foam beads in a swirl of white, green, and blue slime make for a fun planet shape!

BASIC SLIME RECIPE: Crunchy Slime (pg 38-39) • Clear or white PVA glue

MIX-INS: Blue, green & white foam beads • Blue food coloring

SPECIAL STEP/TIP: Mix foam bead colors together for one batch, or make separate batches for each color! Use a clear sphere ornament to mold the Earth shape.

EARTH'S LAYERS SLIME

Earth Day is a popular time to explore the layers of the earth. What better way to do it than with slime!

BASIC SLIME RECIPES: Liquid Starch Slime • Saline Solution Slime • Classic Borax Slime • Clear or white PVA glue

MIX-INS: Food coloring • Tiny rocks

SPECIAL STEP/TIP: Halve 3 slime recipes. Make 6 colors: blue, green, brown, red, orange, & yellow. You can use any of our Unique Slime Recipes for varied textures in your creation!

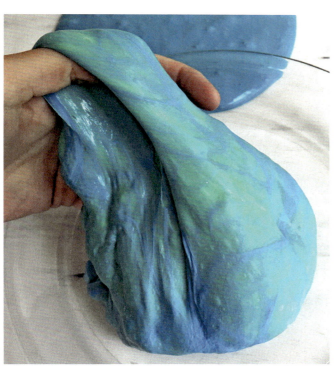

DIY PLANET SLIME

Your kids will have the whole world in their hands with this super squishy, smooth, irresistible slime combination.

BASIC SLIME RECIPE:
Clay Slime (pg 37) • White PVA glue

MIX-INS: Blue or green food coloring • Blue or green soft modeling clay

SPECIAL STEP/TIP:
Make your slime blue or green. Put it in a round pie dish. Break off pieces of blue or green soft clay. Smush to create your planet!

PLANET EARTH SLIME

Celebrate Earth Day with your own globe of glittery slime!

BASIC SLIME RECIPE:
Extreme Glitter Slime (pg 40) • Clear PVA glue

MIX-INS: Blue & green food coloring • Blue & green glitter

SPECIAL STEP/TIP:
Halve the slime recipe. Make ½ green, and ½ blue. Place them side by side then twist together. Squish into a clear sphere ornament and watch it ooze.

EARTH DAY SLIME RECIPES

SPRING SLIME RECIPES

SPRING BUG SLIME

When I think of spring, I think of bugs and butterflies! For an educational activity, pair with an insect or butterfly guide.

BASIC SLIME RECIPES: Liquid Starch Slime • Saline Solution Slime • Classic Borax Slime • Clear PVA glue

MIX-INS: Food coloring, if desired • Plastic bugs and/or butterflies

SPECIAL STEP/TIP: Clear glue works best to see your bugs. Add green food coloring for a bug hunt in the grass!

SPRING MUD SLIME

With a tiny flower pot, this slime will be a big hit with your little gardeners.

BASIC SLIME RECIPES: Liquid Starch Slime • Saline Solution Slime • Classic Borax Slime • Clear PVA glue

MIX-INS: Brown food coloring • Tiny rocks • Fake flowers • Glitter if desired

SPECIAL STEP/TIP: If you are feeling adventurous, experiment with adding some real dirt! You can mix the slime right in the flower pot.

SPRING SLIME RECIPES

FLUFFY RAINBOW SLIME

Got rainy day woes? Brighten it up with this squishy pastel Fluffy Rainbow Slime!

BASIC SLIME RECIPE:
Fluffy Saline Solution Slime • White PVA glue

MIX-INS: All the food coloring colors!

SPECIAL STEP/TIP:
Make 6 half-batches of slime: pink, orange, yellow, green, blue, & purple. Make a white batch for clouds. Line your slimes up and bend them into a fluffy rainbow!

BUTTERFLY SLIME

Studying the butterfly life cycle? Make this gorgeous, sparkling Butterfly Slime part of your activities!

BASIC SLIME RECIPES:
Liquid Starch Slime • Saline Solution Slime • Classic Borax Slime • Clear PVA glue

MIX-INS: Food coloring • Glitter • Butterfly confetti

SPECIAL STEP/TIP:
Coordinate your colors of slime to match your butterfly confetti, then swirl the slimes together.

4TH OF JULY SLIME RECIPES

RED, WHITE & BLUE SLIME

Celebrate your patriotism with red, white, and blue slime!

BASIC SLIME RECIPES: Liquid Starch Slime • Saline Solution Slime • Classic Borax Slime • Clear or white PVA glue

MIX-INS: Red & blue food coloring • Glitter • Confetti

SPECIAL STEP/TIP: If using clear glue, go ahead and add glitter! You could also add red, white, and blue colored sequins to a batch of clear slime!

PATRIOTIC SLIME

Wave your flags! This patriotic themed Parade Slime is the perfect addition to your 4th of July celebration!

BASIC SLIME RECIPES: Liquid Starch Slime • Saline Solution Slime • Classic Borax Slime • Clear PVA glue

MIX-INS: Sequins • Glitter • Confetti • Toothpick flags

SPECIAL STEP/TIP: The Classic Borax Slime will yield the clearest slime to show off your patriotic confetti. Make a parade of flags in your slime!

LEMON/LIME SCENTED SLIME

We love lemonade in the summertime! Enjoy making this refreshing, lemon/lime scented slime for a delicious smelling experience!

BASIC SLIME RECIPE:
Scented Slime (pg 53) • Clear PVA glue

MIX-INS: Lemon & lime flavored gelatin packets • Fruit confetti

SPECIAL STEP/TIP:
Any of your favorite citrus scents will work, but we recommend avoiding sugar free gelatin.

COTTON CANDY SLIME

A favorite summer carnival treat inspired slime. Use shades of light pink and light blue. But remember, no tasting!

BASIC SLIME RECIPE:
Fluffy Saline Solution Slime • White PVA glue

MIX-INS: Red and blue food coloring

SPECIAL STEP/TIP:
Get creative and roll a piece of heavy paper into a pretend stick to wrap your slime around.

SUMMER SLIME RECIPES

SUMMER SLIME RECIPES

UNDER THE SEA SLIME

Celebrate a day by the sea with this gorgeous slime. Learn about the ocean while you play!

BASIC SLIME RECIPES: Liquid Starch Slime • Saline Solution Slime • Classic Borax Slime • Clear PVA glue

MIX-INS: Green & blue food coloring • Glitter • Shells or plastic sea life

SPECIAL STEP/TIP: Make three slimes: blue, light blue, and light green. Spread each slime out next to each other and swirl together. Add plastic sea life too!

STARRY NIGHT SLIME

A shimmery, stargazing slime is perfect for a summer night.

BASIC SLIME RECIPES: Liquid Starch Slime • Saline Solution Slime • Classic Borax Slime • Clear PVA glue

MIX-INS: Blue food coloring • Mini/micro gold star confetti

SPECIAL STEP/TIP: The clear glue base works the best for highlighting the stars. Pull out a constellation guide and use the confetti stars to recreate your favorite constellations.

ALPHABET SLIME

Your ABC slime will have a lot to say when you fill it with alphabet beads.

BASIC SLIME RECIPES:
Liquid Starch Slime • Saline Solution Slime • Classic Borax Slime • Clear or white PVA glue

MIX-INS: Food coloring • Assorted alphabet beads

SPECIAL STEP/TIP:
Use white glue if you want to make an ABC hide and seek! Hunt for letters to create words or for a letter recognition activity.

MINI ERASER SLIME

Mini decorative erasers make it into every back-to-school shopping basket. So, add them to your slime too!

BASIC SLIME RECIPES:
Liquid Starch Slime • Saline Solution Slime • Classic Borax Slime • Clear PVA glue

MIX-INS: Food coloring • Glitter · Mini erasers

SPECIAL STEP/TIP:
Eraser hunt! Pull them out and mush them back in. Use any novelty pack mix of mini erasers to create your own theme.

AUTUMN SLIME RECIPES

APPLE THEMED SLIME

Glittering apple themed slime is perfect for autumn and back to school.

BASIC SLIME RECIPES: Liquid Starch Slime • Saline Solution Slime • Classic Borax Slime • Clear PVA glue

MIX-INS: Red food coloring • Red glitter • Red sequins

SPECIAL STEP/TIP: Make a fun apple themed container complete with construction paper leaves and pipe cleaner stem! Make any color apple slime!

ORANGE PUMPKIN FLUFFY SLIME

Make fluffy orange slime for squishy fall pumpkin slime play!

BASIC SLIME RECIPE: Fluffy Saline Solution Slime • White PVA glue

MIX-INS: Orange food coloring

SPECIAL STEP/TIP: For a deeper orange you will need to add more food coloring. Once your slime is made, dust some orange glitter on top for sparkly pumpkin play!

PUMPKIN SLIME

Make pumpkin slime right inside a pumpkin. Include the pumpkin guts and seeds too!

BASIC SLIME RECIPE:
Liquid Starch Slime • Clear PVA glue

MIX-INS: Sugar pumpkin

SPECIAL STEP/TIP:
Loosen the insides of the pumpkin so that it mixes easily with the slime ingredients. Depending on the amount of pumpkin guts, you may need to remove some before starting your recipe.

FALL LEAVES SLIME

Mimic the colors you see in the trees this fall with gorgeous Fall Leaves Slime.

BASIC SLIME RECIPES:
Liquid Starch Slime • Saline Solution Slime • Classic Borax Slime • Clear PVA glue

MIX-INS: Food coloring • Glitter • Leaf confetti

SPECIAL STEP/TIP:
Twist the slimes together for swirly slime play! Try clear slime and lots of glitter to really show off your leaf confetti!

AUTUMN SLIME RECIPES

HALLOWEEN SLIME RECIPES

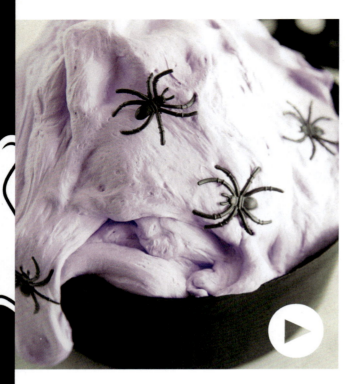

WITCH'S BREW FLUFFY SLIME

Whether you have a little witch or wizard, this fluffy slime activity is perfect for Halloween.

BASIC SLIME RECIPE:
Fluffy Saline Solution Slime
• White PVA glue

MIX-INS: Food coloring
• Plastic spiders

SPECIAL STEP/TIP:
Mix up your fluffy slime in a witch's cauldron! Choose any color you like for your brew.

CLEAR EYEBALL SLIME

Creepy clear slime filled with big eyeballs is sure to create (or inspire) Halloween screams!

BASIC SLIME RECIPE:
Classic Borax Slime • Clear PVA glue

MIX-INS: Plastic eyeballs
• Glitter if desired

SPECIAL STEP/TIP:
Put this slime in a plastic brain mold for extreme Halloween slime play. You can have a friend close their eyes and guess what it is!

HALLOWEEN SLIME RECIPES

VAMPIRE BLOOD SLIME

Make blood red slime Dracula would be proud of! Bleh, bleh bleh!

BASIC SLIME RECIPES:
Liquid Starch Slime • Saline Solution Slime • Classic Borax Slime • Clear PVA glue

MIX-INS: Red food coloring • Glitter if desired

SPECIAL STEP/TIP:
Make sure to add an extra drop or two of food coloring for a deep red slime. Add fake vampire teeth for Halloween play!

CLASSIC HALLOWEEN COLORS SLIME

Choose your favorite Halloween colors to add to a Basic Slime Recipe for seasonal fun.

BASIC SLIME RECIPES:
Liquid Starch Slime • Saline Solution Slime • Classic Borax Slime • Clear PVA glue

MIX-INS: Food coloring • Glitter • Plastic creepy-crawlies & spiders

SPECIAL STEP/TIP:
Add glitter of the same colors or use silver glitter. Plastic spiders, bats, and snakes are fun to mix in!

THANKSGIVING SLIME RECIPES

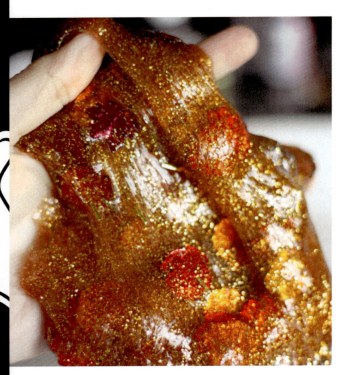

THANKSGIVING CONFETTI SLIME

Glittering slime is perfect for an autumn or harvest time theme.

BASIC SLIME RECIPES: Liquid Starch Slime • Saline Solution Slime • Classic Borax Slime • Clear PVA glue

MIX-INS: Food coloring • Glitter • Thanksgiving confetti

SPECIAL STEP/TIP: Choose colors you feel represent your Thanksgiving day! Add a mix of turkey and leaf confetti with a good splash of gold glitter.

TURKEY FLUFFY SLIME

Our Fluffy Saline Solution Slime is perfect for turkey time!

BASIC SLIME RECIPE: Fluffy Saline Solution Slime • White PVA glue

MIX-INS: Brown food coloring

SPECIAL STEP/TIP: After you make the brown fluffy slime, get crafty with a clear container, complete with pipe cleaner (or construction paper) feathers, googly eyes, and a beak! Gobble, gobble!

HANUKKAH SLIME

Make glittering blue slime for Hanukkah!

BASIC SLIME RECIPES:
Liquid Starch Slime • Saline Solution Slime • Classic Borax Slime • Clear PVA glue

MIX-INS: Food coloring • Glitter • Sequins • Hanukkah themed confetti • Plastic dreidels

SPECIAL STEP/TIP:
You can use the Extreme Glitter Slime (pg 40) to make it really shine. Add lots of sequins for fun.

HANUKKAH CONFETTI SLIME

Make a new slime each night of Hanukkah! With eight nights of slime, the play is nearly endless.

BASIC SLIME RECIPE:
Classic Borax Slime • Clear PVA glue

MIX-INS: Food coloring • Glitter • Sequins • Confetti

SPECIAL STEP/TIP:
Use our Classic Borax Basic Slime Recipe for crystal clear slime and all your confetti will really pop!

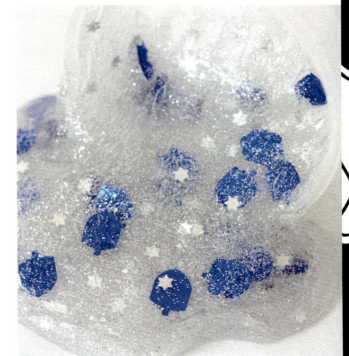

CHRISTMAS SLIME RECIPES

CANDY CANE FLUFFY SLIME

A favorite Christmas treat inspired this festive fluffy slime!

BASIC SLIME RECIPE:
Fluffy Saline Solution Slime
• White PVA glue

MIX-INS: Food coloring

SPECIAL STEP/TIP:
You can make 2 batches of slime, or even 3! Leave one batch white. Color the others your favorite candy cane colors. Twist the colors together to form a fluffy slime candy cane.

TINSEL GLITTER ORNAMENT SLIME

Tinsel glitter is perfect for a festive Christmas touch.

BASIC SLIME RECIPES:
Liquid Starch Slime • Saline Solution Slime • Classic Borax Slime • Clear PVA glue

MIX-INS: Food coloring
• Tinsel glitter

SPECIAL STEP/TIP:
For a gift idea, add the slime to clear sphere ornaments to give to friends or hang on the tree! You can even hide a small plastic figurine inside the slime for a surprise!

GINGERBREAD SCENTED SLIME

Make a wonderfully scented gingerbread man slime, perfect for a cozy winter afternoon.

BASIC SLIME RECIPES: Liquid Starch Slime • Saline Solution Slime • Classic Borax Slime • Clear or white PVA glue

MIX-INS: Gingerbread spices • Glitter • Buttons • Cookie cutters

SPECIAL STEP/TIP: Mix in 1 tbsp of cinnamon and add a ¼ tsp each of ground cloves and ginger. Alternatively you can use gingerbread spice or pumpkin pie spice.

SILVER BELLS SLIME

Add the festive sounds of jingle bells to your slime for Christmas!

BASIC SLIME RECIPE: Silver Slime (pg 46) • Clear PVA glue

MIX-INS: Silver glitter glue • Silver glitter • Jingle bells

SPECIAL STEP/TIP: Use red, gold, or green jingle bells with coordinating slimes too! Jingle bells can be found at the dollar or craft store during the holidays.

CHRISTMAS SLIME RECIPES

KITCHEN SINK SLIME!

Wondering what to do with some leftover slime Mix-Ins? Do you have a little left of a few different things, but not enough to make an individual slime? Try making this Kitchen Sink Slime. A little of this, a little of that, and a whole lot of fun!

BASIC SLIME RECIPES:
Liquid Starch Slime • Saline Solution Slime • Classic Borax Slime • Clear or white PVA glue

MIX-INS:
Anything and everything!

SPECIAL STEP/TIP:
Follow any of the Basic Slime Recipes and during the mix-ins step, go ahead and add your assortment of leftover goodies. Continue with the Basic Slime Recipe directions and you'll have a crazy, one-of-a-kind slime!

LITTLE BINS FOR LITTLE HANDS DOESN'T JUST DO SLIME!

Every week at Little Bins for Little Hands brings an array of awesome science experiments and STEM activities. We LOVE slime, but we also love creating eruptions, building structures, and testing the laws of motion. Hands-on, slimy, gross and exciting science that inspires kids to love science as much as we do is kind of our thing.

So, make sure to stop by and see what we are up to with the changing seasons and holidays. And if you don't want to miss out on our next experiment or slime recipe you can do with your little scientists, subscribe to our weekly newsletter.

WWW.LITTLEBINSFORLITTLEHANDS.COM